Verbal Reasoning

10 Minute Tests

7–8 years

Test 1: Sorting Words 1

Test time: 0 — 5 — 10 minutes

Underline the word in the brackets closest in meaning to the word in capitals.

Example: UNHAPPY (unkind   laughter   <u>sad</u>   friendly)

1. GREAT (large   small   poor   young)
2. SWEET (unkind   sour   sugary   bitter)
3. FOOLISH (wise   sensible   serious   silly)
4. SLIGHT (plump   fair   thin   quick)
5. GNAW (swallow   bite   teeth   food)

Underline the pair of words most similar in meaning.

Example: come, go   <u>roam, wander</u>   fear, fare

6. open, secret   hide, seek   find, discover
7. true, false   knock, thump   black, white
8. neat, tidy   wash, dry   clean, dirty
9. up, down   in, out   distant, far
10. right, left   rush, dash   stop, look

Total ____

Test 2: Selecting Words 1

Test time: 0 — 5 — 10 minutes

Underline two words, one from each group, that go together to form a new word. The word in the first group always comes first.

Example: (hand, <u>green</u>, for)   (light, <u>house</u>, sure)

1. (field, hay, straw) (berry, home, tree)
2. (brick, card, jam) (walk, knife, board)
3. (net, green, slow) (start, ball, grass)
4. (wind, sky, dark) (cloud, mill, leaf)
5. (week, fly, king) (wise, fire, end)

Find the letter which will end the first word and start the second word.

Example: peac (<u>h</u>) ome

6. sac (__) ite
7. boa (__) in
8. car (__) uty
9. fis (__) alf
10. als (__) nto

Total ____

TEST 3: **Sorting Words 2**

Test time: 0 — 5 — 10 minutes

1–5 Write the following words in the correct groups.

Sunday   house   flat   Thursday   cottage

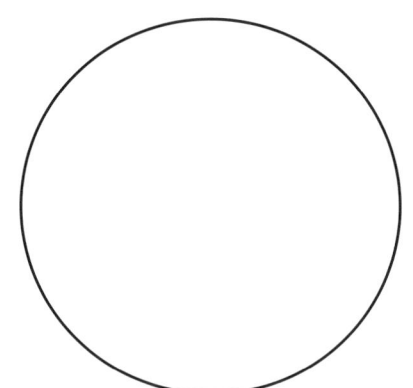

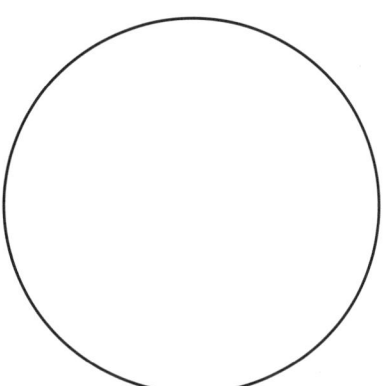

Find a word that is similar in meaning to the word in capital letters and that rhymes with the second word.

Example: CABLE   tyre   ___wire___

6   WET   stamp   _____

7   BEGIN   cart   _____

8   CUT   slim   _____

9   LIE   bib   _____

10 SELECT   cruise   _____

TEST 4: Selecting Words 2

Test time: 0 — 5 — 10 minutes

Which one letter can be added to the front of all of these words to make new words?

Example: <u>c</u> are   <u>c</u> at   <u>c</u> rate   <u>c</u> all

1   ___ host   ___ rain   ___ runt   ___ loom
2   ___ hip   ___ ash   ___ age   ___ ring
3   ___ ion   ___ ease   ___ east   ___ end
4   ___ lug   ___ ink   ___ art   ___ layer
5   ___ trip   ___ eat   ___ old   ___ wing

Complete the following sentences by selecting the most sensible word from each group of words given in the brackets. Underline the words selected.

Example: The (<u>children</u>, books, foxes) carried the (houses, <u>books</u>, steps) home from the (greengrocer, <u>library</u>, factory).

6   All those black and (green, yellow, white) cows produce (grass, milk, parcels) for us to (unwrap, throw, drink).

7   The shark chased the (fish, plane, socks) around the rocks because it was (scared, hungry, pleased).

8   Sonia has a new pink (elephant, dress, slipper) which she wore to the (party, steps, kitchen) on (Saturday, Mars, London).

9   As he (opened, cleaned, threw) the window, the strong (baby, wind, man) blew the papers off the (tree, kitchen, desk).

10   The red (ball, bus, bin) stopped to let the (pencils, passengers, dinosaurs) off at the (end, station, start).

Total

TEST 5: **Selecting Words 3**

Test time: 0 — 5 — 10 minutes

Change the first word into the last word, by changing one letter at a time and making a new, different word in the middle.

Example: TEN   __TIN__   FIN

1   CUP   _____   CAN
2   BAD   _____   RID
3   ZIP   _____   POP
4   SKY   _____   WAY
5   HIM   _____   BIT

Complete the following expressions by underlining the missing word.

Example: Frog is to tadpole as swan is to (duckling, baby, <u>cygnet</u>).

6   Bicycle is to bell as car is to (wheel, horn, door).
7   Ship is to sea as helicopter is to (sky, blades, river).
8   Pond is to fish as hutch is to (boy, rabbit, train).
9   Big is to elephant as small is to (town, monster, mouse).
10   See is to eye as hear is to (nose, mouth, ear).

Test 6: Selecting Words 4

Complete the following sentences by selecting the most sensible word from each group of words given in the brackets. Underline the words selected.

Example: The (<u>children</u>, books, foxes) carried the (houses, <u>books</u>, steps) home from the (greengrocer, <u>library</u>, factory).

1 When we cross the (legs, road, sky) we must (look, eat, draw) carefully to the left and (high, behind, right).

2 Please will you put the (knives, boots, tigers) and (sweets, forks, boxes) on the (table, calendar, fridge) for supper.

3 Susie's cat has (soft, pink, icy) fur and green (ears, eyes, teeth), and he catches (mice, cold, trees).

4 That street lamp (walks, shines, burns) brightly through my bedroom (window, wall, bed) at (day, night, tea).

5 Always (wash, run, soak) your (hands, feet, hair) before meal times.

Remove one letter from the word in capital letters to leave a new word. The meaning of the new word is given in the clue.

Example: AUNT   an insect   ____ant____

6   BITE   a piece   _____
7   PAIR   we breathe this   _____
8   STABLE   a piece of furniture _____
9   RINSE   to get up   _____
10 HOOT   opposite of cold   _____

Test 7: Anagrams 1

Test time: 0 — 5 — 10 minutes

Rearrange the muddled letters in capitals to make a proper word. The answer will complete the sentence sensibly.

Example: A BEZAR is an animal with stripes. ZEBRA

1. Josh slammed the car ROOD as he got out. _____
2. Have you combed your ARIH today? _____
3. His bicycle REYT is punctured. _____
4. Mia has OBRNW eyes. _____
5. Our SEHUO has a blue door and a big garden. _____

Change the first word of the third pair in the same way as the other pairs to give a new word.

Example: bind, hind   bare, hare   but, ___hut___

6. tin, tiny   wax, waxy   man, _____
7. bad, bud   cad, cud   mad, _____
8. lot, loot   met, meet   red, _____
9. part, art   hand, and   fact, _____
10. bat, bad   mat, mad   sat, _____

TEST 8: Anagrams 2

Test time: 0 — 5 — 10 minutes

Answer these questions. The alphabet has been written out to help you.
A B C D E F G H I J K L M N O P Q R S T U V W X Y Z

1. My goldfish's name begins with the eleventh letter of the alphabet.

   Is it: Flash, Jim or Kipper? _____

2. Harriet, Gordon and Isabelle have to stand in alphabetical order, according to their names.

   Who is in the middle? _____

3. Which word begins with the second letter of the alphabet, followed by the fifth, then the first and finally the fourth? _____

4. Which word begins with the third letter of the alphabet, followed by the first, then the seventh and finally the fifth? _____

5. Which of these words contains only letters from the first eight letters of the alphabet?

   dear   belt   head   half _____

6. Make a word from the first, twentieth, third and sixth letters of the alphabet. You will need to rearrange the letters. _____

7–8. If these words were placed in alphabetical order, which word would come:

   first?   can   egg   bed   dog _____
   last?   bet   bat   bit   but _____

Sophie's birthday is on 13th October. Andy's birthday is exactly a week before and Megan's is exactly one week after Sophie's.

9. Andy's birthday is _____
10. Megan's birthday is _____

Time for a break! Go to Puzzle Page 40

Total

TEST 9: Coded Sequences and Logic 1

Test time: 0 – 5 – 10 minutes

If the code for SHAPE is KBMFX, what are the codes for the following words?

1. PEA   _____
2. ASH   _____
3. HEAP   _____

Using the same code, decode these words:

4. KBX   _____
5. FMKK   _____

If a = 2, b = 3, c = 5 and d = 10, find the value of these calculations as numbers.

6. b + c =   _____
7. d − b =   _____
8. c + d =   _____

Using the same values for the letters shown above, give the answers to these calculations as letters.

9. c − b =   _____
10. a + b + c =   _____

Test 10: Coded Sequences and Logic 2

Hal and Will are wearing blue tops.
Will and Brett are wearing shorts.
Brett and Steve are wearing green tops.
Hal and Steve are wearing jeans.

Who is wearing:

1   a blue top and jeans? _____

2   a green top and jeans? _____

3   a blue top and shorts? _____

Class 3 all made snowmen. Flora's snowman was taller than Kara's but smaller than Tiffany's.

4   Who made the smallest snowman? _____

5   Who made the medium-sized snowman? _____

Four of the lockers at school look like this:

top

1	2
3	JOE

bottom

Simon's locker is not in the bottom row. Hanif has a top locker directly over Ali's.

Write down the number of each child's locker.

6   Simon _____   7   Hanif _____   8   Ali _____

If I had 30p more, I would have half as much as my friend who has 80p.

9   How much do I have now? _____

Our break ends at 11:30, and lasts for 20 minutes.

10   What time did it start?   (11:00, 11:10, 11:20)

Test 11: Mixed

Test time: 0 — 5 — 10 minutes

Underline the word in the brackets which goes best with the words given outside the brackets.

Example: word, paragraph, sentence (pen, cap, <u>letter</u>, top, stop)

1. player, goal, ball (pitch, road, shop, tree, sky)
2. lemonade, squash, water (taste, juice, teacup, tap, shop)
3. hutch, stable, pen (chicken, forest, river, barn, town)
4. giraffe, camel, lion (fish, hamster, beetle, bat, zebra)
5. sheet, duvet, pillow (rug, bathroom, oven, house, blanket)

Add one letter to the word given in capital letters to make a new word. The meaning of the new word is given in the clue.

Example: PLAN simple   PLAIN

6. OUR   a number   _____
7. WAS   to clean   _____
8. BOOK   a stream   _____

The classroom clock is 2 minutes fast. It says 12:35 now.

9. What time should the clock say? (12:34, 12:33, 12:32)

My train is 15 minutes late. It should have been here at 9 o'clock.

10. What time is it now? (8:45, 9:05, 9:15)

11

Total

Test 12: Mixed

Rearrange the muddled words in capital letters so that each sentence makes sense.

Example: There are sixty SNODCES __seconds__ in a UTMINE __minute__.

1–2 My favourite LOUROC _____ is NEEGR _____.

3 The schoolchildren ran into the GPARLYNDOU _____ for break.

If the code for LEAST is 12345, what do these codes stand for?

4 1352 _____

5 435 _____

Using the same code, encode these words.

6 SALE _____

7 TEA _____

Complete the following expressions by underlining the missing word.

Example: Frog is to tadpole as swan is to (duckling, baby, <u>cygnet</u>).

8 Grass is to green as sky is to (cloud, rain, blue).

9 Shoe is to foot as glove is to (hand, wool, cold).

10 Climb is to mountain as swim is to (field, river, tree).

TEST 13: **Mixed**

Test time: 0 5 10 minutes

1–5 Write the following words in the correct groups.

cabbage   taxi   bus   car   carrot

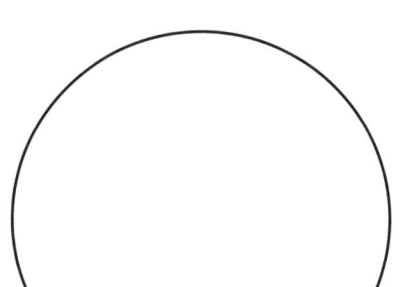 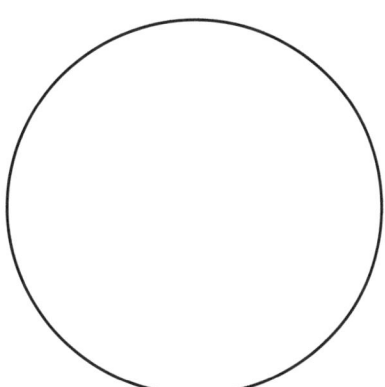

At school lunch one day, Tom and Alice chose sausages. Sara and Vijay chose pie. Tom and Vijay also chose baked beans, and Sara and Alice had salad.

Who chose:

6 sausages and salad? _____

7 pie and baked beans? _____

8 sausages and baked beans? _____

Complete the following sentences by selecting the most sensible word from each group of words given in the brackets. Underline the words selected.

Example: The (<u>children</u>, books, foxes) carried the (houses, <u>books</u>, steps) home from the (greengrocer, <u>library</u>, factory).

9 I keep my (pens, toenails, pencils) sharp by using my sharpener (often, never, tomorrow).

10 When the (train, rain, clock) stops at the (station, hand, house), we must get (into, off, by).

13

Total

Test 14: Mixed

If e = 6, f = 2 and g = 9, find the value of these calculations as numbers.

1. g − e = ___
2. e + f + g = ___
3. e + f + e + f = ___

Find the letter which will end the first word and start the second word.

Example: peac (h) ome

4. tak (___) asy
5. fiz (___) ero
6. was (___) elp
7. sof (___) ake

Answer these questions. The alphabet has been written out to help you.

A B C D E F G H I J K L M N O P Q R S T U V W X Y Z

Put each of these groups of words in alphabetical order. In each group, which word comes last?

8. three, seven, nine, one _____
9. melon, lemon, grapes, orange _____
10. gerbil, fox, kangaroo, jaguar _____

TEST 15: **Mixed**

Test time: 0 — 5 — 10 minutes

Underline the two words, one from each group, which are closest in meaning.

Example: (race, shop, start)   (finish, begin, end)

1 (here, over, on)   (there, under, above)
2 (silent, smooth, bumpy)   (noisy, kind, rough)
3 (near, absent, birthday)   (away, present, wrap)
4 (rubbish, bag, recycle)   (dustbin, litter, bottle)
5 (crooked, simple, plain)   (easy, patterned, straight)

If the code for EARTH is UVWXY, what do these codes stand for?

6 WVX   _____
7 XYU   _____
8 YUVWX   _____

Complete the following sentences by selecting the most sensible word from each group of words given in the brackets. Underline the words selected.

Example: The (children, books, foxes) carried the (houses, books, steps) home from the (greengrocer, library, factory).

9 Joe catches the (mouse, cold, bus) to (school, lunch, bed) every (morning, holiday, birthday).

10 In the park, there is a (house, swing, dog), a slide and a climbing (mountain, frame, newspaper) to play on.

Total

TEST 16: **Mixed**

Test time: 0 – 5 – 10 minutes

Give the missing number in each sequence.

Example: 2 4 6 8 <u>10</u>

1. 1   3   ___   7   9
2. ___   10b   9c   8d   7e
3. 30   35   ___   45   50

Remove one letter from the word in capital letters to leave a new word. The meaning of the new word is given in the clue.

Example: AUNT   an insect   <u>ant</u>

4. PRAM   a male sheep   _____
5. WINK   a liquid used for writing   _____
6. JOINT   to come together   _____

Answer this question. The alphabet has been written out to help you.

A B C D E F G H I J K L M N O P Q R S T U V W X Y Z

7. John has his music exam in the month beginning with the fifteenth letter of the alphabet. Which month is it?   _____

If the letters of the following words are placed in alphabetical order, what is the third letter of each word? The alphabet has been written out to help you.

A B C D E F G H I J K L M N O P Q R S T U V W X Y Z

8. APPLE   _____
9. PATCH   _____
10. DANCES   _____

Time for a break! Go to Puzzle Page 40

Total

TEST 17: **Mixed**

Test time: 0 — 5 — 10 minutes

Underline the two words which are the odd ones out in the following groups of words.

Example: black   <u>king</u>   purple   green   <u>house</u>

1   snug   fire   radiator   cosy   warm
2   eye   ear   sock   nose   shirt
3   pea   orange   blue   daisy   red
4   cup   spoon   mug   beaker   fork
5   November   May   Monday   Friday   July

I live in the village of Shrimpcomb. The road from the village to Dawnhill is twice as long as the road out to Triptown. The road from the village to Frantley is half as long as the road out to Triptown.

6   Which town is closest to Shrimpcomb?   _____
7   Which town is furthest from Shrimpcomb?   _____

Complete the following expressions by underlining the missing word.

Example: Frog is to tadpole as swan is to (duckling, baby, <u>cygnet</u>).

8   Curry is to food as milk is to (cow, white, drink).
9   Cushion is to sofa as pillow is to (chair, bed, sleep).
10 Black and white is to zebra as orange and black is to (tiger, striped, chair).

17

Total

Test 18: Mixed

Find the letter which will end the first word and start the second word.

Example: peac (h) ome

1 sta (__) isk
2 mor (__) ven
3 fas (__) ook

Rearrange the muddled words in capital letters so that each sentence makes sense.

Example: There are sixty SNODCES __seconds__ in a UTMINE __minute__.

4–5 The NAIR _____ pattered on the windowpane during the STRMO _____.

6 'OWH _____ do you do?' said the stranger.

If v = 3, w = 5, y = 10 and z = 4, find the value of these calculations as numbers.

7 v + z + w = ___
8 y − z − w = ___

Using the same values for the letters shown above, give the answers to these calculations as letters.

9   w + w = ___
10 y − v − z = ___

Test 19: Mixed

Underline the word in brackets closest in meaning to the word in capitals.

Example: UNHAPPY (unkind laughter <u>sad</u> friendly)

1. TIGHT   (baggy loose small soft)
2. PILLOW   (bed cushion feather chair)
3. STAMP   (seal letter post foot)
4. ENTIRE   (part most half whole)
5. HORSE   (stable pony cow field)

Give the missing number in each sequence.

Example: 2 4 6 8 <u>10</u>

6. 16   14   12   ___   8
7. 4   40   5   50   ___
8. 100 ___ 300 400   500

Complete the following sentences by selecting the most sensible word from each group of words given in the brackets. Underline the words selected.

Example: The (<u>children</u>, books, foxes) carried the (houses, <u>books</u>, steps) home from the (greengrocer, <u>library</u>, factory).

9. (Catch, Talk, Bite) the (stone, ball, hill), Maya, and (run, throw, eat) it to Tony.
10. The old (cat, man, tree) picked up his walking (dog, sock, stick) and closed the (book, door, box) behind him.

Test 20: Mixed

A B C D E F G H I J K L M N O P Q R S T U V W X Y Z

Make words from these letters of the alphabet. You will need to rearrange the letters.

1. eighth, first, fifth and twenty-second letters   _____
2. twenty-fifth, twenty-sixth, first and twelfth letters   _____
3. seventh, first, fifth and thirteenth letters   _____

Add one letter to the word given in capital letters to make a new word. The meaning of the new word is given in the clue.

Example: PLAN   simple   ___plain___

4. SHOT   to call out   _____
5. POT   a pimple   _____
6. WINE   to moan   _____

In a test of 20 questions, each question was given one mark. From the information below, work out how many marks each child received.

Gwen got half the answers right.

David got three more marks than Jamal but two fewer than Gwen.

Lewis got six questions wrong.

7. Gwen   _____
8. David   _____
9. Jamal   _____
10. Lewis   _____

TEST 21: Mixed

Underline the pair of words most similar in meaning.

Example: come, go   <u>roam, wander</u>   fear, fare

1. hard, soft   correct, right   find, lose
2. skin, bone   tooth, claw   hair, fur
3. back, front   fasten, tie   pull, push
4. still, calm   stormy, frosty   float, sink
5. first, last   below, under   same, opposite

Fill in these crosswords with the words below.

6.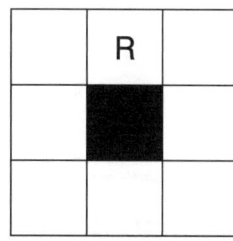

   ORB   BOX
   FOX   OFF

7.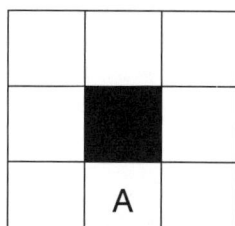

   TRY   SIT
   SOB   BAY

8.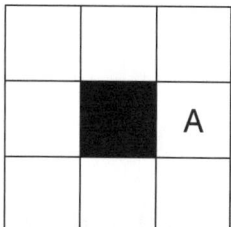

   LIP   TOT
   LET   PAT

Michael is older than Marta and Marta is older than Brian.

9. Who is the oldest?   _____
10. Who is the youngest?   _____

Test 22: Mixed

Find the letter which will end the first word and start the second word.

Example: peac (h) ome

1. laz (___) olk
2. kic (___) ing
3. fil (___) ilk

If 10th August was a Friday, work out the answers to these questions.

4. What would be the date of the next Friday? _____
5. What day of the week was 7th August? _____
6. What date would the next Monday after 10th August be? _____

Give the missing number in each sequence.

Example: 2   4   6   8   <u>10</u>

7. 16   19   22   25   ___
8. ___   5y   6x   7w   8v
9. 30   ___   20   15   10
10. 7   11   15   ___   23

Test 23: Mixed

Find the letter which will end the first word and start the second word.

Example: peac (h) ome

1. bak (___) nvy
2. fee (___) oaf

If h = 7, i = 3, j = 10 and k = 4, give the answers to these calculations as letters.

3. h + i = ___
4. h − i = ___
5. i + k = ___

Find a word that is similar in meaning to the word in capital letters and that rhymes with the second word.

Example: CABLE   tyre   <u>wire</u>

6. CHAT   walk   _____
7. NARROW   win   _____
8. STREET   code   _____
9. TOOTH   rang   _____
10. EAGER   bean   _____

Answers

Bond 10 Minute Tests 7–8 years: Verbal Reasoning

Test 1: Sorting Words 1

1. large
2. sugary
3. silly
4. thin
5. bite
6. find, discover
7. knock, thump
8. neat, tidy
9. distant, far
10. rush, dash

Test 2: Selecting Words 1

1. strawberry
2. cardboard
3. netball
4. windmill
5. weekend
6. k
7. t
8. d
9. h
10. o

Test 3: Sorting Words 2

1–5 Homes: house, flat, cottage
     Days: Sunday, Thursday
6. damp
7. start
8. trim
9. fib
10. choose

Test 4: Selecting Words 2

1. g
2. w
3. l
4. p
5. s
6. white, milk, drink
7. fish, hungry
8. dress, party, Saturday
9. opened, wind, desk
10. bus, passengers, station

Test 5: Selecting Words 3

1. CAP
2. BID
3. PIP
4. SAY
5. HIT
6. horn
7. sky
8. rabbit
9. mouse
10. ear

Test 6: Selecting Words 4

1. road, look, right
2. knives, forks, table
3. soft, eyes, mice
4. shines, window, night
5. wash, hands
6. bit
7. air
8. table
9. rise
10. hot

Test 7: Anagrams 1

1. DOOR
2. HAIR
3. TYRE
4. BROWN
5. HOUSE
6. many
7. mud
8. reed
9. act
10. sad

Test 8: Anagrams 2

1. Kipper
2. Harriet
3. bead
4. cage
5. head
6. fact
7. bed
8. but
9. 6th October
10. 20th October

Test 9: Coded Sequences and Logic 1

1. FXM
2. MKB
3. BXMF
4. SHE
5. PASS
6. 8
7. 7
8. 15
9. a
10. d

Test 10: Coded Sequences and Logic 2

1. Hal
2. Steve
3. Will
4. Kara
5. Flora
6. 2
7. 1
8. 3
9. 10p
10. 11:10

Bond 10 Minute Tests 7–8 years: Verbal Reasoning

Test 11: **Mixed**

1. pitch
2. juice
3. barn
4. zebra
5. blanket
6. FOUR
7. WASH
8. BROOK
9. 12:33
10. 9:15

Test 12: **Mixed**

1–2. colour green
3. playground
4. LATE
5. SAT
6. 4312
7. 523
8. blue
9. hand
10. river

Test 13: **Mixed**

1–5. Vegetables: cabbage, carrot
Vehicles: taxi, bus, car
6. Alice
7. Vijay
8. Tom
9. pencils, often
10. train, station, off

Test 14: **Mixed**

1. 3
2. 17
3. 16
4. e
5. z
6. h
7. t
8. three
9. orange
10. kangaroo

Test 15: **Mixed**

1. over, above
2. bumpy, rough
3. absent, away
4. rubbish, litter
5. simple, easy
6. RAT
7. THE
8. HEART
9. bus, school, morning
10. swing, frame

Test 16: **Mixed**

1. 5
2. 11a
3. 40
4. ram
5. ink
6. join
7. October
8. L
9. H
10. D

Test 17: **Mixed**

1. fire, radiator
2. sock, shirt
3. pea, daisy
4. spoon, fork
5. Monday, Friday
6. Frantley
7. Dawnhill
8. drink
9. bed
10. tiger

Test 18: **Mixed**

1. r
2. e
3. t
4–5. rain, storm
6. how
7. 12
8. 1
9. y
10. v

Test 19: **Mixed**

1. small
2. cushion
3. seal
4. whole
5. pony
6. 10
7. 6
8. 200
9. Catch, ball, throw
10. man, stick, door

Test 20: **Mixed**

1. have
2. lazy
3. game
4. shout
5. spot
6. whine
7. 10
8. 8
9. 5
10. 14

Test 21: **Mixed**

1. correct, right
2. hair, fur
3. fasten, tie
4. still, calm
5. below, under

6.

O	R	B
F		O
F	O	X

7.

S	I	T
O		R
B	A	Y

8.

L	I	P
E		A
T	O	T

9. Michael
10. Brian

Test 22: Mixed

1. y
2. k
3. m
4. 17th August
5. Tuesday
6. 13th August
7. 28
8. 4z
9. 25
10. 19

Test 23: Mixed

1. e
2. l
3. j
4. k
5. h
6. talk
7. thin
8. road
9. fang
10. keen

Test 24: Mixed

1. LET
2. SEA
3. LAST
4. swan
5. meat
6. were
7. them
8. sugar, tea
9. bread, birds, garden
10. brother, buttons, shirt

Test 25: Mixed

1. shallow
2. huge
3. empty
4. cloudy
5. follow
6. k
7. r
8. ZQD
9. VZQV
10. XQVXZ

Test 26: Mixed

1. star
2. seat
3. hero
4. BLACK
5. FILL
6. PEAR
7. SINK
8. B
9. C
10. D

Test 27: Mixed

1. RAT, TAR
2. ARE, EAR
3. SAW, WAS
4. LOW, OWL
5. TUB, BUT
6. s
7. e
8. w
9. most
10. belt

Test 28: Mixed

1. bit
2. but
3. been
4. sheep
5. chickens
6. goats
7. floor
8. eight
9. animal
10. freezing

Test 29: Mixed

1. stardust
2. bookmark
3. rainbow
4. moonlight
5. suitcase
6. harm
7. seen
8. shed
9. THERE
10. BEAR

Test 30: Mixed

1. Sanjay
2. Nick
3. Chris
4. rap
5. hat
6. rain
7. tall
8. cute
9. pray
10. reap

Test 31: Mixed

1. FOOT
2. SNOW
3. PLAY
4. BLACK
5. FIRE
6. 12th November
7. Monday
8. man
9. sea
10. wash

Test 32: Mixed

1. 397
2. 438
3. 8734
4–5. moon   stars
6–7. park   summer
8. <u>sun</u>, wind
9. <u>worm's</u>, spider's
10. <u>pens</u>, pencils

Test 33: Mixed

1. m
2. r
3. s
4. t
5. b
6. 10:25
7. 40
8. feel
9. bare
10. plan

Bond 10 Minute Tests 7–8 years: Verbal Reasoning

Test 34: Mixed

1. C
2. B
3. D
4. 4663
5. 4732
6. 3285
7. 9561
8. park, ducks, pond
9. red, white, pink
10. chocolate, flavour

Test 35: Mixed

1. SEW
2. FAR
3. SUN
4. HUT
5. DIE
6.
7.
8. tries
9. draw
10. tusk

Test 36: Mixed

1. stone
2. ditch
3. sand
4. law
5. 19th April
6. Monday
7. 27th April
8. <u>cow</u>, cat
9. <u>off</u>, on
10. <u>vegetables</u>, fruits

Test 37: Mixed

1. pond, boat
2. sign, wind
3. time, just
4. wearing, not
5. icing, candles
6. day, finishes
7. dog, coat, white
8. cross, road, busy
9. boiled sweets
10. chocolate bars

Test 38: Mixed

1. MN
2. TS
3. X7
4. JL
5. P3
6. word
7. can
8. pill
9. win
10. and

Test 39: Mixed

1. a
2. h
3. y
4. 4
5. 1
6. 2
7. rope
8. vine
9. pinch
10. grow

Test 40: Mixed

1. <u>wind</u>, nose
2. <u>walls</u>, trees
3. <u>train</u>, chair
4. <u>ears</u>, eyes
5. bed
6. car
7. had
8. JCK
9. KNPK
10. KNJJ

Puzzle 1

1. TOP
2. GAP
3. NUT
4. CAT

Puzzle 2

new, old
cheap, expensive
thick, thin
silent, noisy
near, far
wrong, right
true, false

Puzzle 3

1. THEN, TRAY, TRIP, TRUE, TOWN, TWIN
2. CHIP, CALL, COIL, CROWN, CAGE, CRIB
3. SOLD, SELF, STAR, SEAT, SLID, SWAN, SHOP, SPOT
4. PLAY, PRAY, PRIM, PINK, PAIR

Puzzle 4

Bottom tunnel

Puzzle 5

1. north
2. south, west
3. east, north
4. south, south
5. north, east

TEST 24: **Mixed**

Test time: 0　5　10 minutes

If the code for STEAL is 79145, what do these codes stand for?

1 519 _____

2 714 _____

3 5479 _____

Find the four-letter word hidden at the end of one word and the beginning of the next word. The order of the letters may not be changed.

Example: The children had bat<u>s and</u> balls. ___sand___

4 Amir does want to go after all. _____

5 Come at four o'clock. _____

6 He likes to have a shower every day. _____

7 Jane greeted the man. _____

Complete the following sentences by selecting the most sensible word from each group of words given in the brackets. Underline the words selected.

Example: The (<u>children</u>, books, foxes) carried the (houses, <u>books</u>, steps) home from the (greengrocer, <u>library</u>, factory).

8 Do you like (sugar, soap, hair) in your (book, tea, chair)?

9 My dad put some (milk, bread, stones) out for the (cats, bears, birds) that made a nest in our (garden, kitchen, car).

10 My baby (bubble, brother, sister) always has his (spoons, buttons, teeth) undone on his (shirt, socks, pram).

Time for a break! Go to Puzzle Page 41

Total

Test 25: Mixed

Underline one word in the brackets which is the most opposite in meaning to the word in capitals.

Example: WIDE (broad, long, <u>narrow</u>, motorway)

1. DEEP (dark, flat, pool, shallow)
2. TINY (small, huge, little, speck)
3. FULL (crowded, whole, near, empty)
4. CLEAR (cloudy, bright, open, safe)
5. LEAD (guide, follow, walk, train)

Find the letter which will end the first word and start the second word.

Example: peac (h) ome

6. lic ( ) nee
7. bea ( ) oof

If the code for MATCH is DQVXZ, what are the codes for the following words?

8. HAM _____
9. THAT _____
10. CATCH _____

TEST 26: Mixed

Find the four-letter word hidden at the end of one word and the beginning of the next word. The order of the letters may not be changed.

Example: The children had ba<u>ts and</u> balls.   __sand__

1. The Browns are just arriving now.   _____
2. A mouse ate the piece of cheese.   _____
3. He rode his bicycle slowly.   _____

Add one letter to the word given in capital letters to make a new word. The meaning of the new word is given in the clue.

Example: PLAN   simple   __plain__

4. BACK   a colour   _____
5. ILL   to top up   _____
6. PEA   type of fruit   _____
7. INK   part of a kitchen   _____

Here is a chart showing Annie's chest of drawers. Using the information below, work out which clothes she keeps in each drawer.

top
| SOCKS |
| B |
| C |
| D |
bottom

Annie's socks are kept in the top drawer. Her shirts are between the socks and the jumpers. The trousers are under the jumpers.

8. shirts ____   9. jumpers ____   10. trousers ____

TEST 27: **Mixed**

Test time: 0 — 5 — 10 minutes

Underline the two words which are made from the same letters.

Example: TAP   PET   <u>TEA</u>   POT   <u>EAT</u>

1	RAT	ROT	TAR	PAW	RAW
2	RED	ARE	ROD	ADD	EAR
3	SAT	TAB	SAW	WAS	BOW
4	LOW	WHO	SOW	SLY	OWL
5	HUB	TUB	HUT	BUT	HUG

Find the letter which will end the first word and start the second word.

Example: peac (<u>h</u>) ome

6 mis (___) oap
7 wid (___) ggs
8 dra (___) eed

Underline the words that have their letters in alphabetical order. The alphabet has been written out to help you.

A B C D E F G H I J K L M N O P Q R S T U V W X Y Z

| 9 | gift | most | half | ages |
| 10 | rise | fear | nose | belt |

Total

Test 28: Mixed

Change the first word of the third pair in the same way as the other pairs to give a new word.

Example: bind, hind   bare, hare   but, ___hut___

1 let, lit   set, sit   bet, _____
2 can, ban   cow, bow   cut, _____
3 kite, bite   kill, bill   keen, _____

Here is a diagram of part of our local farm.

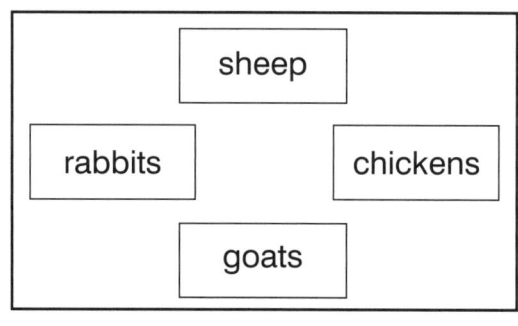

4 Which animals are in the north of the farm?   _____
5 Which animals are in the east of the farm?   _____
6 Which animals are in the south of the farm?   _____

Complete the following expressions by underlining the missing word.

Example: Frog is to tadpole as swan is to (duckling, baby, <u>cygnet</u>).

7 Picture is to wall as carpet is to (floor, ceiling, room).
8 Six is to seven as seven is to (eight, odd, number).
9 Feather is to bird as fur is to (animal, coat, frog).
10 Hot is to cold as boiling is to (freezing, warm, saucepan).

TEST 29: **Mixed**

Test time: 0 — 5 — 10 minutes

Underline two words, one from each group, that go together to form a new word. The word in the first group always comes first.

Example: (hand, <u>green</u>, for) (light, <u>house</u>, sure)

1 (reed, star, clock)   (bark, dust, food)
2 (left, tall, book)   (stairs, water, mark)
3 (blue, rain, sharp)   (bow, part, stick)
4 (moon, bright, sand)   (light, end, spark)
5 (red, bag, suit)   (apple, rag, case)

Find the four-letter word hidden at the end of one word and the beginning of the next word. The order of the letters may not be changed.

Example: The children had bat<u>s and</u> balls. ___sand___

6 Both armies are fighting.   _____
7 Please enter the cinema.   _____
8 She dances very well.   _____

If the code for BREATH is 413659, what do these codes stand for?

9   59313   _____
10 4361   _____

Test 30: Mixed

Four boys compared their bedrooms.

Nick and Matt have two windows, while Chris and Sanjay have one window.

Nick and Sanjay have blue walls and a few posters, while Chris and Matt have red walls and many posters.

1. Which boy has one window and a few posters? _____
2. Which boy has two windows and blue walls? _____
3. Which boy has red walls and one window? _____

Remove one letter from the word in capital letters to leave a new word. The meaning of the new word is given in the clue.

Example: AUNT   an insect   ___ant___

4. WRAP   knock   _____
5. HEAT   headwear   _____
6. DRAIN   wet weather   _____
7. STALL   high   _____

Underline the one word which **cannot be made** from the letters of the word in capital letters.

Example: STATIONERY   stone   ration   <u>nation</u>   noisy

8. CUTTING   tug   tint   gut   cute
9. PREACH   pray   race   care   harp
10. SLIPPER   ripe   pies   reap   pile

TEST 31: **Mixed**

Test time: 0 — 5 — 10 minutes

Find a word that can be put in front of each of the following words to make new, compound words.

Example: CAST FALL WARD POUR ___DOWN___

1 BALL PATH STEP PRINT _____
2 FLAKE BALL MAN BOARD _____
3 TIME PEN GROUND MATE _____
4 BOARD CURRANT BIRD SMITH _____
5 WORK PLACE LIGHT WOOD _____

If 6th November was a Saturday, work out the answers to these questions.

6 What was the date of the following Friday? _____
7 What day of the week was 1st November? _____

Change the first word of the third pair in the same way as the other pairs to give a new word.

Example: bind, hind   bare, hare   but, ___hut___

8 cap, can   tap, tan   map, _____
9 tool, too   band, ban   seal, _____
10 bell, well   band, wand   bash, _____

30

Test 32: Mixed

If the code for BADGE is 83497, what are the codes for the following words?

1. AGE _____
2. DAB _____
3. BEAD _____

Rearrange the muddled words in capital letters so that each sentence makes sense.

Example: There are sixty SNODCES _seconds_ in a UTMINE _minute_.

4–5 The rocket zoomed up in the sky towards the MONO _____ and RASST _____.

6–7 The flowers in the RKAP _____ bloomed all MSUREM _____.

Change one word so that the sentence makes sense. Underline the word you are taking out and write your new word on the line.

Example: I waited in line to buy a <u>book</u> to see the film. _ticket_

8. The sun blew the washing on the line back and forth. _____
9. The fly was caught in the worm's sticky web. _____
10. Sharpen your pens over the bin, please. _____

Test 33: Mixed

Which one letter can be added to the front of all these words to make new words?

Example: <u>c</u> are   <u>c</u> at   <u>c</u> rate   <u>c</u> all

1   ___ other   ___ at   ___ ill   ___ eat
2   ___ are   ___ ash   ___ oast   ___ ice
3   ___ eat   ___ upper   ___ lip   ___ and
4   ___ hat   ___ hump   ___ rip   ___ he
5   ___ at   ___ old   ___ east   ___ eaten

My PE lesson started at 10:20 and finished at 11:00. I arrived 5 minutes late.

6   At what time did I arrive?   _____
7   How many minutes did the lesson last?   (45, 30, 40)

Change the first word of the third pair in the same way as the other pairs to give a new word.

Example: bind, hind   bare, hare   but, <u> hut </u>

8   look, leek   stool, steel   fool, _____
9   car, care   pan, pane   bar, _____
10 four, pour   fox, pox   flan, _____

TEST 34: **Mixed**

Test time: 0 — 5 — 10 minutes

Suki's cat had four kittens. Kitten A and Kitten B were black and white. Kitten C and D were ginger. Kitten A and Kitten D had green eyes. Kitten B and Kitten C had yellow eyes.

Which kitten had:

1 yellow eyes and ginger fur? _____

2 yellow eyes and black and white fur? _____

3 green eyes and ginger fur? _____

These words have been written in code, but the codes are not under the correct words.

WOOD	WIDE	DEAR	FROM
9561	4663	4732	3285

Match the correct codes to the words.

4 WOOD _____

5 WIDE _____

6 DEAR _____

7 FROM _____

Complete the following sentences by selecting the most sensible word from each group of words given in the brackets. Underline the words selected.

Example: The (<u>children</u>, books, foxes) carried the (houses, <u>books</u>, steps) home from the (greengrocer, <u>library</u>, factory).

8 On Sundays we often go to the (park, school, table) to feed the (spiders, ducks, buses) at the (zoo, pond, tree).

9 (Red, Blue, Green) paint mixed with (white, yellow, orange) paint makes the colour (painting, pink, wall).

10 (Chocolate, Hot, Green) ice cream is my favourite (friend, colour, flavour).

Test 35: Mixed

Test time: 0 — 5 — 10 minutes

Change the first word into the last word, by changing one letter at a time and making a new, different word in the middle.

Example: TEN ___TIN___ FIN

1 SEA _____ DEW
2 FAT _____ FOR
3 FUN _____ SUM
4 HAT _____ GUT
5 PIE _____ DID

Fill in the crosswords with the words below.

6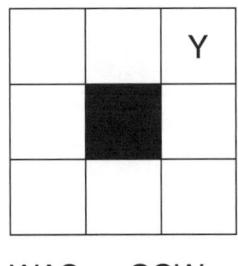

WAS   COW
YES   CRY

7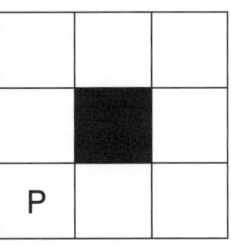

NOW   PIN
PAW   PUP

Underline the one word which **cannot be made** from the letters of the word in capital letters.

Example: STATIONERY   stone   ration   <u>nation</u>   noisy

8   THIRST   hit   shirt   tries   stir
9   WONDER   draw   word   done   wore
10 DUSTER   red   stud   rust   tusk

Test 36: Mixed

Change the first word of the third pair in the same way as the other pairs to give a new word.

Example: bind, hind bare, hare but, ___hut___

1. team, steam lime, slime tone, _____
2. wish, dish wart, dart witch, _____
3. lad, land had, hand sad, _____
4. row, raw sow, saw low, _____

If 13th April was a Wednesday, work out the answers to these questions.

5. What was the date of the following Tuesday? _____
6. What day of the week was 11th April? _____
7. What was the date exactly a fortnight after 13th April? _____

Change one word so that the sentence makes sense. Underline the word you are taking out and write your new word on the line.

Example: I waited in line to buy a <u>book</u> to see the film. ___ticket___

8. Mary's cow has had four kittens in that basket. _____
9. As it is too dark to see, please turn off the light and continue. _____
10. Strawberries and cherries are my favourite vegetables. _____

TEST 37: **Mixed**

Test time: 0 5 10 minutes

Find and underline the two words which need to change places for each sentence to make sense.

Example: She went to <u>letter</u> the <u>write</u>.

1 The pond floated on the boat.
2 The sign blew the wind over.
3 He was time in just to catch the train.
4 That man is wearing not matching socks.
5 Jade's cake had ten red icing and pink candles.

Complete the following sentences by selecting the most sensible word from each group of words given in the brackets. Underline the words selected.

Example: The (<u>children</u>, books, foxes) carried the (houses, <u>books</u>, steps) home from the (greengrocer, <u>library</u>, factory).

6 Our school (night, day, team) (finishes, starts, kicks) at 4pm.
7 Moira's (scarf, pen, dog) has a shaggy (button, coat, carpet) which is black and (green, freezing, white).
8 When we walk to school we (eat, cross, cycle) one small (sign, road, bridges) and four (busy, pavement, rush) roads.

A likes candyfloss and chocolate bars.
B likes boiled sweets and liquorice.
C likes liquorice and sherbet.
D likes candyfloss and sherbet.
E likes chocolate bars and liquorice.
F likes boiled sweets and chocolate bars.

9 What do B and F both like? _____

10 What do A, E and F all like? _____

Total

Test 38: **Mixed**

Test time: 0 — 5 — 10 minutes

Fill in the missing letters. The alphabet has been written out to help you.
A B C D E F G H I J K L M N O P Q R S T U V W X Y Z

Example: AB is to CD as PQ is to RS

1. TU is to VW as KL is to ____.
2. ZY is to XW as VU is to ____.
3. T3 is to U4 as W6 is to ____.
4. AC is to DF as GI is to ____.
5. M9 is to N7 as O5 is to ____.

Remove one letter from the word in capital letters to leave a new word. The meaning of the new word is given in the clue.

Example: AUNT   an insect   ant

6. SWORD   made up of letters   _____
7. CLAN   a tin container   _____
8. SPILL   a tablet   _____

Change the first word of the third pair in the same way as the other pairs to give a new word.

Example: bind, hind   bare, hare   but, ___hut___

9. kind, kin   pant, pan   wine, _____
10. feel, eel   meat, eat   sand, _____

37

Test 39: Mixed

Find the letter which will end the first word and start the second word.

Example: peac (h) ome

1. are (___) nts
2. bat (___) eel
3. onl (___) ard

In a pet shop there are four cages in a row containing different small animals. From the information below, work out which type of animal is in each cage.

1	2	RATS	4

The mice are not in a cage at the end of the row.

The gerbils are next to the rats but not next to the guinea pigs.

4. The gerbils are in cage ___.
5. The guinea pigs are in cage ___.
6. The mice are in cage ___.

Underline the one word which cannot be made from the letters of the word in capital letters.

Example: STATIONERY stone ration <u>nation</u> noisy

7. PATTERN rent rope part neat
8. DRIVING vine grind ring grid
9. PENCILS slice snip pinch spine
10. ORANGE near grow ogre gone

Test 40: Mixed

Change one word so that the sentence makes sense. Underline the word you are taking out and write your new word on the line.

Example: I waited in line to buy a book to see the film.   __ticket__

1   Don't sniff, Jane, please blow your wind.   _____

2   In Autumn many leaves fall from the walls.   _____

3   My grandmother sits in her train by the fire.   _____

4   She cried and her ears filled with tears.   _____

Answer these questions. The alphabet has been written out to help you.
A B C D E F G H I J K L M N O P Q R S T U V W X Y Z

5   Make a word from the second, fifth and fourth letters of the alphabet.

_____

6   Make a word from the first, third, and eighteenth letters of the alphabet. You will need to rearrange the letters.   _____

7   Make a word from the first, fourth and eighth letters of the alphabet. You will need to rearrange the letters.   _____

If the code for TRIAL is KPCNJ, what are the codes for the following words?

8   LIT   _____

9   TART   _____

10 TALL   _____

Puzzle 1

Alphabet Pyramids

Spell a word by using one letter from each row of the pyramid. Start with the top letter and work downwards. One has been done as an example.

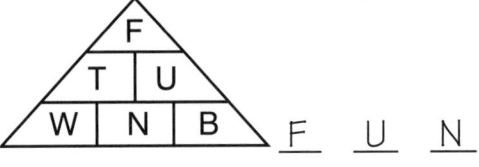

1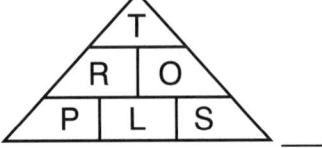

3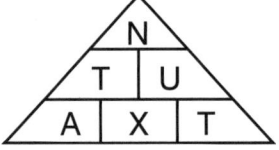

2

4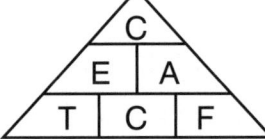

Puzzle 2

Match the Opposites

Draw a line to connect the words in each column that mean the opposite. Watch out, there are a few extra words that do not match! The first one has been done as an example.

black ———————	**white**
skinny	noisy
new	inexpensive
cheap	quiet
thick	thin
long	expensive
silent	right
near	false
distant	old
wrong	boiling
true	far

Puzzle 3

Word Wall

Shade the bricks that make a word that starts with the letter in bold. Here is an example.

B	OLD	ASH	FIN	END
	ARM	ALL	EAR	OWN

T	HEN	RAY	RIP	SET	RUE
	RID	BAT	OWN	WIN	LIP
C	HIP	ALL	HIM	OIL	RAT
	END	ROW	AGE	BUT	RIB
S	OLD	ELF	ARM	TAR	EAT
	RIB	LID	WAN	HOP	POT
P	LAY	RAY	RIM	TAN	INK
	OFF	FOR	RAN	AIR	LET

Puzzle 4

Tunnel Trouble

Rowena Rabbit needs to return to her babies in their burrow deep beneath the hill.
Help her to choose the right tunnel.
Only by following the path with the logical sequence of numbers can she make it safely home.

Which one is it, the top, middle or bottom tunnel? _____

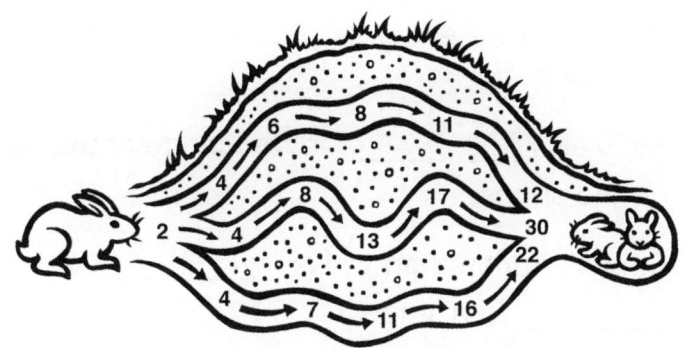

Puzzle 5

Adrian's Journey

Here is a map of the area where Adrian lives. He lives near the park and is allowed to walk to the shops, the pond and school using the paths in the park.

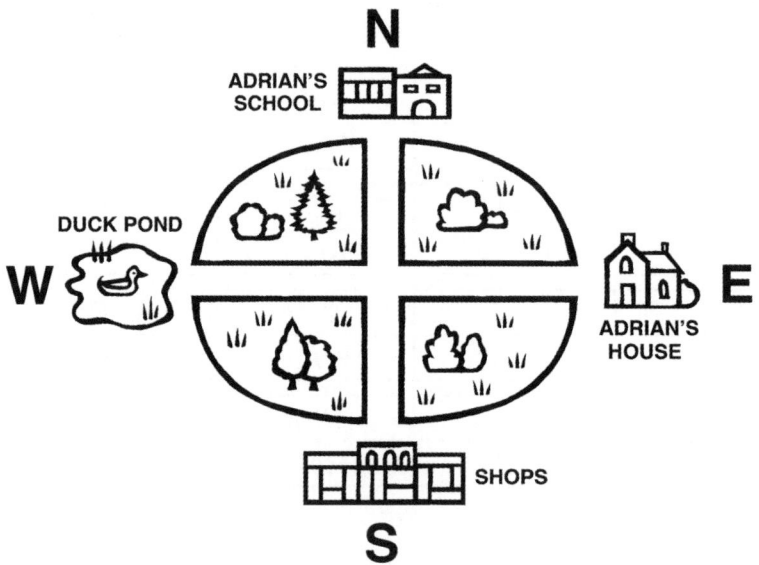

Using the points of the compass, write the direction Adrian has to travel to do the following journeys. The first one has been done for you.

1. One morning, Adrian walks to school by going ___west___ to the centre of the park and then _____ to school.

2. In break time, their teacher takes Adrian and his class to the pond to feed the ducks and draw sketches of them. They travel _____ from school to the centre of the park and then _____ to the pond.

3. Going back to school, they walk _____ to the centre of the park and then _____ to school.

4. After school, Adrian walks _____ to the centre of the park and then to the _____ to the shops.

5. Having bought a snack, Adrian then walks _____ to the centre of the park and then _____ to his house.

Progress Grid

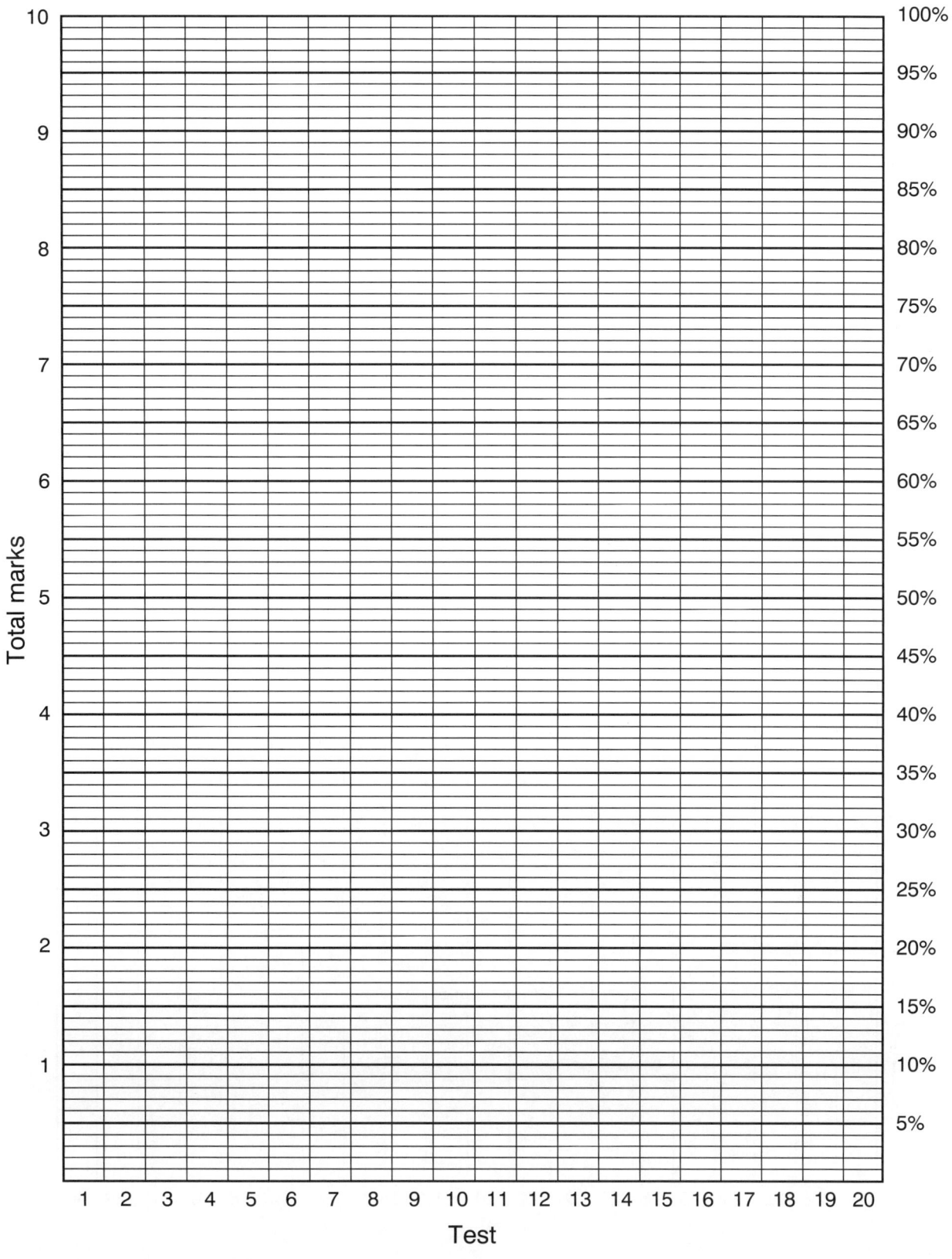

Progress Grid

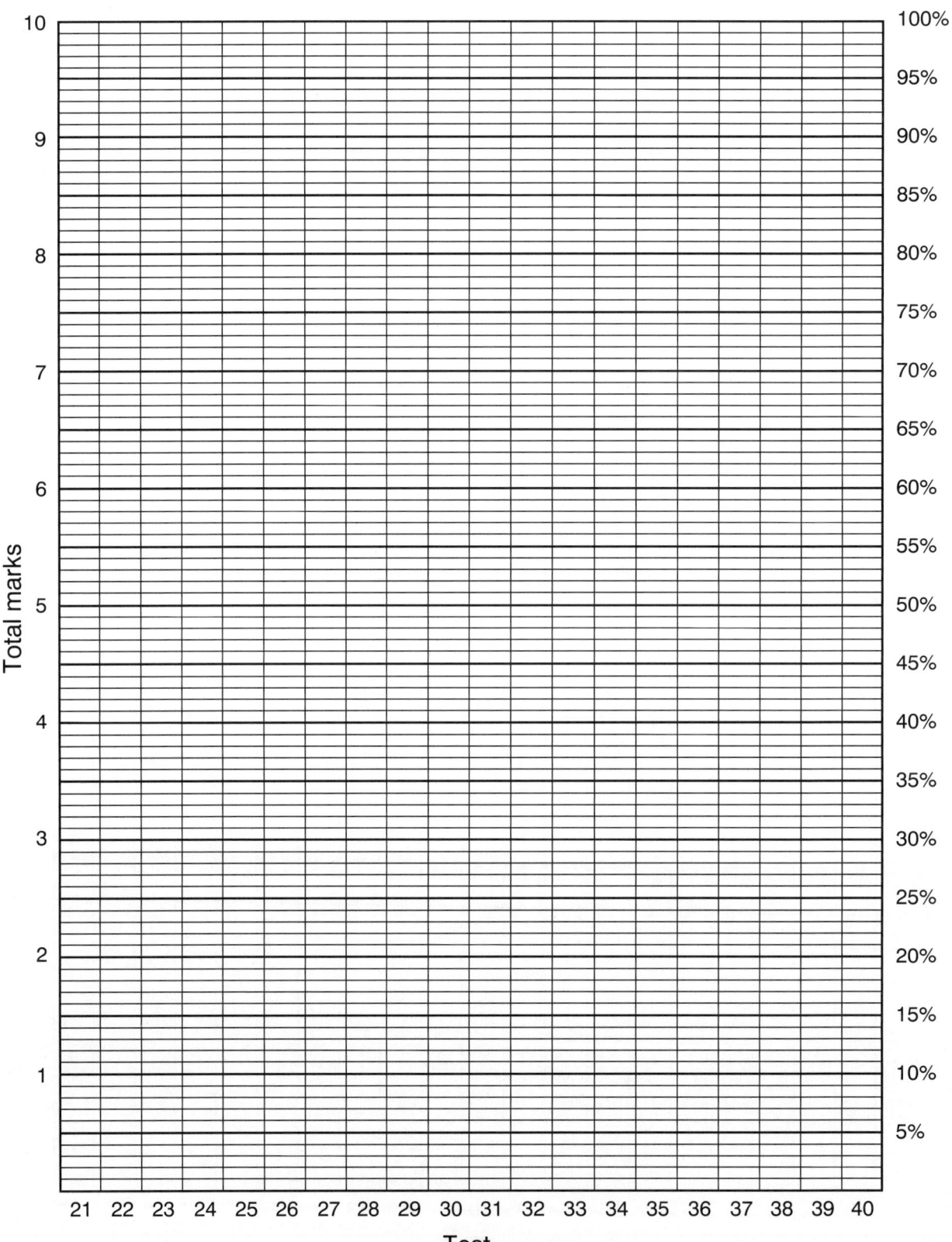